W9-DDQ-163

Ya Gotta
OPEN 'EM
Before You Can
CLOSE 'EM

SMART SELLING

Strategies to Reinvent the Sales Process

GERRY LAYO

PSCI Publishing
La Jolla, California

Copyright © 2003 Gerry E. Layo

All rights reserved. No part of this publication may be reproduced or transmitted in any form or by any means, or stored in a database or retrieval system, without the prior written permission of the publisher.

Third Printing 2012

Published by:
PSCI Publishing
5842 La Jolla Corona Drive
LaJolla, CA 92037

Project Management, Rewriting, Editing, and Design: Clarity Coaches, Inc.
Cover Design: Ad Graphics Inc., Tulsa OK
Printed in the Unites States by Mennonite Press, Inc, Newton, Kansas

Cataloging in Publication Data
Layo, Gerry E.
You Gotta Open 'Em Before You Can Close 'Em:
SMART SELLING – Strategies to Reinvent the Sales Process
ISBN Number: 978-0-9712126-2-6

Dedication

When the initial run of Smart Selling was printed 10 years ago,
I had dedicated this book to my three best friends;
Dia, my wife and partner for 20 years and my beautiful
daughters, Khloe and Madisyn who are so close to "leaving
the nest" that my heart hurts just thinking about it. In that
dedication, I mentioned that Dia was (and continues to be) my
very best friend in this life and that Khloe and Madi were my
heart and my soul for whom I get up to fight every day, hoping
to continue to be their hero.

Since that time, we have welcomed my son Cooper into this
world and he keeps my focus on setting the right example
daily for hard work, perseverance, and respect that needs to
be instilled in a young man today. The youthful enthusiasm
and spirit that he brings to our family adds additional spark
and smiles to our lives every day. Together with the women in
my family, he inspires me to be a better man, a better father, a
better friend, and a better listener.

To all of you, I dedicate this, the 3rd printing of Smart Selling!

Acknowledgments

There are so many people who have in some way contributed to this book that it is hard not to go back into the early days of my life to describe the impact that teachers, coaches, friends, family, etc., have had on me. However, there are not enough pages in the book, so I will be brief:

My deepest and heartfelt gratitude:

To Shelly Frank for helping me write this book. Without Shelly, the book would have taken another couple of years. She played a major role in the creation of this book and in finding a voice that would introduce you to me.

To all the sales and sales management specialists who have provided a pathway to excellence before my time. I use your words liberally in my seminars and examples. Thank you deeply for my attitude of gratitude.

To Jack Daly for being my mentor, my friend, and my jumpstart into this business of speaking and training. Without a doubt, Jack, you have pointed out to me that anything I set my mind to can be done. As I continue on in this life, I look forward to sharing more and more moments together as we *suck the marrow out of the bone of life.*

And to all of you in the business of sales. What you do takes courage, strength, commitment, attitude, skills, activity, action, and persistence every day. I am proud to serve you all in my written and spoken word as I work in this field. I hope that you all find at least *one gold nugget* in these works that will help you achieve more and get the results that you so richly deserve.

SMART SELLING
Strategies to Reinvent the Sales Process

By Gerry Layo

Foreword

This book is for you, the sales professional. Whether you have been in the field of sales for one week, one month, or several decades, this book is designed with you in mind.

If you are looking for deep meaning, I must apologize in advance. If you are looking for quick fixes, shortcuts, and/or *secrets* to cut years off your learning curve, again, you are out of luck. What I can promise you (in these pages) are street-tested tactics based upon years of sales success. I like to call all of this stuff BFOs or Blinding Flashes of the Obvious. There is nothing new here. There is nothing earth shattering in these pages. Just good sales philosophies and methodologies from a pretty good sales guy turned sales trainer.

I caution you on a few things: First, don't confuse simplicity with a lack of depth. I have the good fortune to work with literally thousands of salespeople every year, and way too often many of you are looking way too deep for answers that are right on the surface. Second, don't let me lose you on the fact that some of the examples that I use may not seem to fit with your current type of sales job description. You are a salesperson, for goodness sake! Use your talents of relationship development (the key word in that is to *relate)* and adapt the examples to you and your current sales career! Just don't let yourself off the hook by saying, "This doesn't relate to me" or "Gerry doesn't understand the subtleties of *my* business." Your business is sales, and regardless of what you sell, the length of your sales cycle, the average size of your sale, or whether it is retail, wholesale, inside, outside, phone, Internet, door-to-door, or *whatever,* THIS STUFF APPLIES if you do your best to make it fit your situation. Lastly, don't feel that you need to read this book from cover to cover and then move on. Write in it! Dog-ear it! Hi-Lite the good stuff! Make notes in the margins! Use this book like you would a good article, a textbook (one you own), or a series of short stories. But for Heaven's sake, *USE IT!!*

I had a ball with this, my first effort at the written word in book form. I hope that you will take to heart the words in these pages and put some of them into use to help you build your respective book of business. I promise you that I will follow up this book with others as time and my career allow. I have a lot to say, and some of it is even worth reading!

As I continue on in my career as a speaker, trainer, coach, and now author, I hope to get a chance to work with you on building your sales career. I have been very fortunate in my life to be blessed with many solid mentors, coaches, teachers, and colleagues from whom I have gained many of the insights that I have shared in these pages. I have read the words of hundreds of other authors in the field of sales and self-development, and I have attended hundreds of seminars in person or through audio training. If some of the words that you read in this book sound familiar, it is because they come from a mixture of all of these people, with my own special sauce added for flavor. I treat all that I have learned with great reverence, and have worked hard to credit those throughout these pages where credit is due. Where I may have been remiss in doing so, please forgive me and look at such examples as pure flattery of the originators.

As a sales professional, I urge you to continue to seek out knowledge and experience through a multitude of resources. There are way too many salespeople in today's marketplace who do not seek to grow themselves before they seek to grow their incomes. It is those salespeople who will provide to you, their competition, all of the customers that you deserve.

Sell well, my friends!

Contents

Introduction:
Sales Isn't Easy, but It's Simple

EXECUTIVE SUMMARY

We've all read some great sales and sales management books. And – if we're good – from time to time we brush up, take a personal inventory, and see how we can alter the course of our current paths. That's what you're doing right now. Whether you're a seasoned sales professional, a sales manager, a CEO, or are just starting out, you've chosen to pick up this book and add some tools to your toolbox.

We chose this career. We chose it for the things that come from it, such as a virtually unlimited income. We chose it to be validated when people do "buy" us, like us, and trust us, and then because of that, get involved with our products or services.

It takes some special elements to create success in sales. It takes guts, intelligence, persistence, faith, commitment, attitude, skills, and action to do what we do every day. And that takes courage – courage to get out of your comfort zone, do something that frightens you every day, and commitment to constant change and growth.

In this book, I review some "blinding flashes of the obvious" – things that you probably already know but have forgotten as you face new challenges in your career. Nothing in this book is rocket science. However, without goals, the proper attitude, a solid view of the mechanics, and consistent effort, you'll never see the blinding flashes. Learn to play the GAME:

- **Goals**
- **Attitude**
- **Mechanics**
- **Effort**

● ●

Sales is an interaction between two people. It's the persuasion business. It's the communication business.

● ●

Whether you're an outside or inside salesperson, a customer service rep, or a business owner, you're in sales. Sales is just an interaction between two people. It's the persuasion business. It's the communication business. It's a matter of getting your ideas moved over to me so that I will buy them. Someone, some-how, somewhere will be making these sales, so it might as well be you. You need to know how to make your strategies more accurate than ever. Being in the right place at the right time with the right message is not enough. How you separate your-self from all the other salespeople will determine your success.

● ●

The first thing you have to sell is yourself.

● ●

Whenever you walk into a prospective customer's office, you are selling three things, not one. Your company and its history – its track record, its marketing materials, its rave reviews, its glow-ing endorsements – don't mean anything until you've made the first sale. This is my main focus in this book: The first thing you have to sell is yourself. The last thing you should be trying to sell is price, because as long and you're in the game, it does not matter once you make the first two sales.

It has been said that we need to work smarter, not harder. I believe we need to work smarter *and* harder. Let's agree not to continue to focus on the close. Relationships make all the difference. People will do business with those they know and trust. Change your focus and you will change your results. By continuing to concentrate on closing deals, you'll never fully understand the method by which you will close bigger and better deals, which is, again, to sell in this order:

- You
- Your company and product
- Price

In that order! I believe that understanding comes with continuing education and that continuing education begins with a concept that I call KERP:

- Enhancing your personal and professional *Knowledge*
- Learning from *Experience*, both your and others'
- Identifying and multiplying your *Resources*
- Having a solid *Philosophy* of total responsibility.

● ●

We cannot expect our results to change unless we are willing to change first.

● ●

I'm going to ask you to turn inward. Face yourself and say, "I'm going to be the one to make that change." We cannot expect our results to change unless we are willing to change first.

Many people say that a salesperson has to be a good talker, but there's something we need more than talking skills, and that's listening skills. We need to ask questions and listen.

We tend to focus on what we're going to say, how we're going to put our presentation together, and how we're going to deliver our value proposition. But if I'm going to sell to you, I don't know *how* to construct a value proposition for you because I don't know what you value. I don't know what your motivators are – your pains, your fears, your desires. I don't know what your buying style is or how you make decisions. I won't know what your challenges are unless I ask. Once I find those things out, you're going to tell me how to do business with you. You're going to tell me how to earn your business if I ask questions, but until then, I'm just another sales guy.

I see sales as simply a transfer of trust. If you don't trust or like me, that pretty much guarantees that you're not going to do business with me. So why worry about selling my product if I haven't yet sold myself?

● ●
I don't believe we close deals; I believe we open customers.
● ●

There is a simple trick to this: Stop trying to close deals. I don't believe we close deals; I believe we open customers. Once a customer is open to buying from you, you earn the right to gain that business on a day-to-day basis. You do this through your actions, through what you say, the questions you ask, the way you listen, the way you respond.

I'm going to give you a lot of information in this book. All I want is for you to come away with one or two gold nuggets that you can take to your business and put into action. What are you going to act on? If you can commit to acting on it, I'll commit to making sure that I deliver on the value.

I am pretty firm in my commitment to give you something, no matter how small, that you're going to be able to use to get better results and make more money. If nothing else, I hope to wake something up in you and light a fire that can lead you into the next few weeks until you choose to either let that fire die down or to stoke the flames. I ask you to take responsibility for this! You chose the field of sales. The tough thing about sales is that if you don't "kill" you don't "eat." The good thing about sales is that when you "kill" you eat better than most. YOU CHOOSE!

PART I
················
What Are You Selling?

PART I:
WHAT ARE YOU SELLING?

Sales Is a Transfer of Trust:
Hey Buddy – Wanna Buy a Watch?

You're a salesperson; you've heard it all: "Oh, you're in sales, huh? Great. Gee, look at the time; I gotta go." We deal with the image of the used-car salesman in the plaid sports coat, and with, "Hey buddy – wanna buy a watch?"

• •

Salespeople are the most important individuals in the world economy. Without what we do, no one has a job.

• •

I believe that salespeople are the most important individuals in the world economy. I believe that without what we do, no one has a job! You don't HAVE a company without selling something first. That person who picked up the phone and made the first call to sell the first product *made* your company. The person who goes out into the world is the point man for your organization. If you are that point man, you're the most important person, in my eyes, in your organization.

• •

A sale is simply a transfer of trust.

• •

A sale is simply this: It's a transfer of trust. If you trust me, it doesn't guarantee that you're going to do business with me, but if you don't trust me, that pretty much guarantees that you're *not* going to do business with me. Your liking me doesn't guarantee that you're going to buy from me, either, but if you don't like me, that pretty much guarantees that I'm out the door. So why am I worried about selling my financial services, my ad space, my telephone systems, my chemicals? If you don't like me, what are the chances that I'm going to make the sale? If you don't trust me, why would you do business with me? If you don't trust me, you don't trust my price, my products or services, or their reliability.

The concept of transferring trust doesn't apply just to outside sales. If you work on the phones from the inside providing customer service to existing clients, the most important thing that you can do – because customer service is also sales – is to continually sell yourself as a client advocate inside your organization. That comes with communication, with a GREAT attitude, and from being there for the client. It comes from listening … asking questions and listening! The best way to transfer trust is to get people to buy *you*. And do you know the best way to accomplish that? Get them talking about their favorite subject: Themselves. Their business, their hobbies, their families.

Sales isn't easy, but it's simple. Sales is just an interaction between two human beings. It's the persuasion business. It's the communication business. It's getting my ideas moved over to you so that you will buy them. Most of all, it's a transfer of trust.

The Three Sales

My whole premise here is based on you, the sales professional. I believe there are three sales to be made every time we enter the field of battle – not necessarily the first time we meet a prospect, but EVERY time we meet our customers and clients. By the "field of battle" I mean sales; who doesn't have competitors? Is there anybody in sales who doesn't have other people calling on their customers trying to take business away from them? The sales are going to be made, and they're going to be made by somebody. It might as well be you. There are three sales that have to be made every time you see your prospects:

- You
- Your Company, Product, or Services
- Your Price

Notice that price comes last. Many salespeople think that if they had better prices they'd make more sales. If you've ever said that before, do yourself a favor and never say it again! NOBODY CARES!

If you don't make the first two sales, all that will matter is price.

I'm going to make a couple of strong statements: Your company and its history – its track record, its glossy marketing materials, its rave reviews, its glowing endorsements – don't mean anything until you've made the first sale. Customers might make price objections, but price doesn't matter unless you succeed in making the first two sales. But if you don't make the first two sales, *all* that will matter is price.

Here's another strong statement: NOBODY WANTS WHAT YOU'RE SELLING.

Whatever your product or service is, I don't want it, because it's just a mechanism to get me to the benefit that I want. Have you ever gone to a hardware store to buy a drill? Guess what? You didn't go there to buy a drill; you went to get a hole. Do you go to the dentist for drilling, pulling, and scraping? Those are *features* of a trip to the dentist. But the *benefits* of a trip to the dentist are great: strong, healthy teeth and a brighter smile.

So you see, it's a lot easier to sell benefits than it is to sell your product. And the better we can do that based on our customers' needs, the more we can charge for our products. *So don't think about being able to sell more if your product was cheaper; think about selling better so your product can command a higher price!* If we do a better job selling ourselves, we don't have to negotiate. We don't have to apologize for our price. We can hold it up proudly, and people will say, "I can see why, with talent like you, your company is the most expensive in town. But I don't want to do business with anybody else. I want you." Do you get that kind of response from your customers?

You are your product – a combination of the way you walk, the way you talk, the way you act, the way you communicate. It's important to have the company, the products, the services, the marketing materials, the endorsements, the referrals list … the whole nine yards. Those elements are necessary when you're structuring a company. Having a solid value proposition, communicating value in your product, and making sure it's a good return on investment are important too. But my point is that you won't get a chance to talk about those things until you make the first sale.

THE FOUR CS

A successful sales transaction has four key elements. Two relate directly to the attitude of the salesperson (top sales professionals are defined by their attitudes; I'm going to cover a lot about that later) and two relate to the customer.

- Confidence
- Credibility
- Contribution
- Comfort

A salesperson's confidence and credibility are founded in knowledge and based on preparation. Confidence and pride in your company and in your product are things that prospects can see in your eyes and hear in your voice.

When you're selling, remember to get the other party involved! Ask questions and listen to what the customer has to contribute – buying is not a spectator sport; it's a participatory sport. Comfort is a feeling that your customers must have before they buy from you. They must believe that you have their best interests at heart. If they're uncomfortable, chances are they're not going to go through with the transaction.

OPEN CUSTOMERS, DON'T CLOSE DEALS

When most of us learned sales, we were taught to get out there and get a deal. We were taught the FAB points of our products or services – the features, advantages, and benefits. We were told to get out there and wow 'em with what we do and how we do it. We learned to sell this way:

- Do a quick introduction then

- Qualify prospects to see if they're customers or not (The old-school method of qualifying was to put a mirror under their noses; if it fogged up, we'd pitch them.)

- Give them a canned presentation, which we were taught like this: "On this page you go through this and then flip it over. On this page you go through this, and this page you go through this. Look around the room, make a joke, pause, and laugh, ha, ha, ha. Go back to the page."

- When we give the canned presentation, there's something natural that's going to come up: Objections. So we are taught to "overcome objections": "If they say this, you say that. They say this, you say that." It's a Ping-Pong match.

- At the end you take off the salesman's hat and put on the closing jacket because it's time to jam it down their throats. Then we pull out the 43 power closes.

Do you want to learn how to sell more? I'm going to give you a simple trick: STOP TRYING TO CLOSE DEALS. If I asked a room full of 1,500 salespeople to name the one thing I could help them with the most, 1,480 of them would say, "Teach me how to close more business." I'm going to teach you how to sell more, but I'm going to teach you by telling you to stop asking me that. You'll notice that I stay away from the word *close,* because I don't believe we close deals; I believe we **open** customers. Once a customer is open to doing business with you, you earn the right to gain that business on a day-to-day basis. You do it through your actions, through what you say, the questions you ask, the way you listen, and the way you respond.

● ●
**Stop worrying about closing the deal.
You've got to open your customers first.**
● ●

STOP WORRYING ABOUT CLOSING THE DEAL. You've got to open your customers first. If you open your customers and then walk them through a tailor-made, customized value proposition, the only natural thing for them to do is to buy from you. Stop worrying about getting there first. Open them up and earn the right to do business with them. That's closing!

KEY POINTS: WHAT IS SELLING?

- Without what salespeople do, no one has a job.
- Selling is a transfer of trust.
- There are three sales that need to be made every time:
    1. You
    2. Your Company, Product, or Service
    3. Your Price
- If you don't make the first two sales, all that will matter is price.
- Nobody wants what you're selling, so it's easier to sell benefits than it is to sell your product.
- Remember the four Cs of selling: Confidence, credibility, contribution, and comfort.
- STOP TRYING TO CLOSE DEALS!!!
- Once a customer is open to doing business with you, you earn the right to gain that business.
- Someone, somehow, somewhere will make the sale; it might as well be you.

PART II

· · · · · · · · · · · · · · · · ·

How Do You Sell It?

PART II:
HOW DO YOU SELL IT?

What do most salespeople sell? Features: We push the features because when we are hired, one of the first things to happen is that we go into product knowledge training. Often we participate in a complex, intensive, three-part training program:

1. "Here are your cards."

    2. "There's your territory."

        3. *Big Kiss* 💋 "Good luck, baby!"

And we're supposed to go out and do something with this. At that point, we're like lumberjacks. We're going out into the forest every day, swinging our axes, trying to knock down trees. And there are other lumberjacks out there swinging their axes too.

What I hope to do is help you take that ax off your shoulder and put it down on the grindstone and sharpen it. Abraham Lincoln said, "If I had ten days to chop down a tree, I'd spend the first eight days sharpening my ax." What usually happens in sales, though, is that we go out and do the same thing day in and day out. Pick up the phone, day in and day out, call the same people, say the same thing over and over, sounding exactly like the last twenty-five people who called. At the end of the day, we get call reluctance … that phone gets heavy. Soon it weighs 200 pounds, then 300 pounds. We end up going into the forest with a bowling ball tied to the end of a big stick, and we are just bludgeoning the trees. This is hard work! "This isn't what I signed up for! Sales is supposed to be exciting. It's supposed to be fun. But the door is being slammed in my face. People are canceling appointments; they're canceling orders. And, man, this bowling ball is getting heavy!" It is at this point that we start becoming a little "call reluctant" and feeling "burnt out."

Here's another way of looking at it. Let's say I'm going to try and sell to you; you're my prospect. I'm going to sit in front of your desk, and I'm going to say, "Thanks for getting together with me today."

You're going to sit behind your desk and think, *Another sales guy. How long is this going to take? Let's get through this.*

If I'm a typical salesperson, that's probably how I'm going to feel about it, too, because I'm going to "show up and throw up." That's what salespeople do when they say, "Let me tell you about me, blah, blah, blah …." Professional? I don't think so!

● ●

There's an imaginary brick wall between us when we meet. I can't sell through a brick wall.

● ●

I believe there's an imaginary brick wall between us when we meet. The rules are that I can't sell through this brick wall. It's thick. It's long. It's tall. I can't go around it. I can't climb over it. I can't dig under it. The only way that I can do business is if

I can transfer trust, but I can't do that through a brick wall. So what do I have to do? I have to break down that wall. I've got to start removing those bricks. I do that by asking questions, because I want to show you that I care about you and I care about your business. I care about your particular needs, not about customers *like* you, but *you*. Here's the cool part about this: As

my customer, YOU'VE GOT TO PLAY BY THE SAME RULES, so now we start transferring a little bit of trust. I start asking you about your business: "How'd you get involved with this? Tell me a bit about your business."

You, the customer, might say, "I've got four or fives choices out there, because you've got competitors; why would I choose to do business with you?" Those are questions, and questions remove bricks. Together we have a shot at lowering that wall, and only then have I got a shot at talking (or you listening) about my company, and then about my products.

What usually happens is that salespeople go out into the field and say, "Thanks for getting together with me." Then they open up the laptop and say, "Let me show you the magical presentation I've got in here. This is why you'll do business with me. The answer is in this little black box."

And they wonder why prospects say, "Well, thanks for coming in. Let me kick it around. Let me run that up the flagpole. Let me crunch some numbers. Let me think about it. I'll get back to you." All of that nonsense is a nice way of saying, "No! You didn't do your job. I don't know you! You came in and opened up a book or a laptop and you showed me charts and figures and stuff. I don't know *you*! I don't know you well enough to know whether I trust you or not. And most importantly, you don't know me!"

A lot of people over-think sales. But it's as basic as this: You talk to your prospects, and if they like you and understand what you're talking about … and if you make some kind of bond with them and find out what they're doing, then they'll take a look at your company. If it's not too messed up, they'll give you a shot. Stop focusing on your products and your company so much. I'm not saying that we don't need to know our products, and that we don't need to know what our company does and what its history and success stories and competitors are. We're going to talk about all those things, but first and foremost, work on the most important product that you have: You, the salesperson.

● ●

The only thing that we have the ability to change is ourselves.

● ●

And do you know what? You're the easiest thing to work on. The only thing that we have the ability to change is ourselves. No matter how much we bellyache about what's going on around us – the customer's hesitance and what's going on inside the customer's business – we can do absolutely nothing about those things until we turn inward and decide how WE can be different. Don't say, "If I had a better product, I'd sell more." You *are* your product, so go ahead and get a better product. You've got to sell YOU before you sell your product or your company, and then finally, price.

•••••••••••••••••••••••••••••••••••

Ask yourself,
"Why would *I* do business with me?"

•••••••••••••••••••••••••••••••••••

When your prospect is getting ready to make a commitment to buy from you, it's not just a matter of how much it's going to cost for them to come over and do business with you. If they've got a good relationship with their current vendor, doing business with you requires a change. It's a question of how much pain it's going to cause to sever that relationship. So ask yourself these questions all the time: "Why would *I* do business with me?" Look yourself in the eye before you go on every call and say, "Would *I* do business with me? How do I look today? How's my attitude today?" Oh, yes, you're darn right – I'm going to talk about attitude. It's coming up. Here are a couple of concepts to help you sell more effectively: KERP (Knowledge, Experience, Resources, Philosophy,) and GAME (Goals, Attitude – there it is – Mechanics, Effort).

KERP

This is an acronym coined by a previous coach and mentor of mine, Ron Sutton. There are no new concepts – just a new way of thinking…of putting things together so that when we GET IT, WE REALLY GET IT!

Knowledge

Think of everything you need to know before you make a sale: Your products and pricing, your customers, your competition. Top sales reps are constantly looking for sources of knowledge. They're always asking questions. Do you know how you can find out the most about how to sell your product better and how

---

to keep your customers? Do you know where you can get the best answers? Ask your existing clients. Ask them why they do business with you; what they like about it? Also ask what they *didn't* like about doing business with you. Ask what you could have done better. Ask your clients what is most important to them. But don't leave it up to them to come up with answers! Ask specific, closed – rather than open-ended – questions: "What's most important, A, B, or C? Do you prefer this or that?" Lead them somewhere.

● ●

If you aren't training,
you aren't gaining.

● ●

If I'm always learning, I'm confident that I'm growing. If I'm growing, I know that I'm doing a good job for you. I say to sales managers, "If you aren't training, you aren't gaining." The minute I stop training my sales team is the minute they start to go backward, not just to stagnate. In business you don't stand still. You're either going forward or backward. If you are gaining knowledge, you're going forward. Increase your knowledge by tapping into the other elements of KERP: knowledge, experience, resources, and your philosophy. Work on all of these every day.

● ●

Turn to other individuals
in your organization and ask,
"What would you do here?"

● ●

Experience

Life's too short to experience everything by yourself! How often do you get together with other sales professionals and compare notes? Do you turn to other individuals in your organization and ask, "What would you do here? I'm facing a challenge, and I seem to keep running into a wall. How would you overcome that?" Do you ask your boss that kind of question? Do you think you're going to look stupid if you do? I think you'll look foolish if you don't, and you'll also keep failing. Reach out; life is too short to experience everything single-handedly. Benefit from the experience of those around you, especially if they've been around a little longer and they're producing more.

How does one get more experience? Typically, business owners let their salespeople go out and get their own bumps. After all, you learn more from your failures than from your successes. Well, darn it, go ask somebody else about his or her failures instead of having to suffer your own! I'd rather learn from YOUR mistakes than from mine! That makes learning a lot easier. You have to learn from everything. You have to tap into the experience that's around you.

Resources

What resources can you tap into to expand your knowledge? You're using one right now – you're reading a book. Hopefully, it will turn on a couple of lights for you. Hopefully, you'll find a gold nugget or two that you can act on. Other resources include:

- Your customers; ask them questions
- Seminars
- Tapes; listen while you drive

- Industry magazines (both your industry and your customers')
- Top salespeople
- Your peers
- The Internet

These should be blinding flashes of the obvious!

Your competitors are a resource; go to them and ask questions. Don't be afraid of them.

Your competitors are a resource too; go to them and ask questions. And do you know that if you go to them, your competitors might just ask, "Hey, how do you do that?" Share knowledge with them, and invite them into your business. Often you don't get until you give. Don't be afraid of your competitors. If you're that much better, it doesn't matter if they know what you're doing. I'll share with my competitors anytime: "Here's exactly what I do and how I do it. But nobody does it with my special sauce, so good luck!"

When you learn something that really turns on a light for you, *write it down*.

There are resources everywhere that can help you sharpen your ax so you can go out there and chop down trees. How many do you use every day? Ask yourself this question at the end of the day for thirty days: "In what area did I grow today and what resources helped me?" When you learn something that really turns on a light for you, *write it down* to ensure that you use that knowledge. I've got 136 red notebooks stacked in my closet. For the past 14 years, every night before I go to bed – it's the last thing I do at night – I write down what I learned that day. It forces me to review my day and pick up something. It might have been something I read. It might have been something a customer told me. It might have been something my five-year-old said: "Daddy, you're sure happy a lot." Whatever it may be, write it down. Resources are all around us; it's just a matter of whether we're going to use them or not.

• •
Ask your existing clients why they do business with you.
• •

Philosophy

I'm going to ask you to adopt a philosophy of total responsibility (just like Brian Tracy taught us to do). Whatever's going on with your personal book of business as a salesperson within a company – good, bad, or ugly – I'm going to ask you to take responsibility as the only person who can change it. Don't look to your company for more training. Don't look to your company for more marketing materials, better territory, more clients, better clients, better price structures, or anything else. Turn inward, face yourself, and say, "If it's going to happen, it's up to me. I'm going to be the one to make that change." We cannot expect our results to change unless we're willing to change first.

Let's say your average monthly sales are twenty-five units. One month, you come out of the gate and knock off forty-eight units. What might you say? "Look what I did. Man, I was *on* this month. NOBODY was telling me 'no.' Look what *I* did. Me. *Me*." The next month, you sell thirteen units, and you say, "Nobody's buying. What can I do?" But good or bad, *you* did it. Good *or* bad. Sometimes the wheel rolls our way, and sometimes it rolls the other way, but the minute we stop pushing that wheel, we've got an opportunity to get run over. The only thing you can change, for worse or for better, is the person who stares at you in the mirror every morning when you brush your teeth. If you're not happy with your production, what can you do to change yourself?

For business owners and CEOs, the message is slightly different. I don't want you to say, "I don't know why my salespeople aren't more productive." It's not their fault. *You* have to take the responsibility. If you want them to change, you're the only person who can change their attitude, their skills, and their activity. You're the person who can make them decide whether they *get to* come to work in the morning or *have to* come to work in the morning.

Whomever you are, whether you're a business owner or a salesperson, adopt a philosophy of total responsibility. That's what's going to give you the ability to change.

• •

**It's not up to customers to come to us;
it's up to us to get customers. It's not
up to our competition to leave us alone;
it's up to us to separate ourselves
from the competition.**

• •

Do you know what they say in the old school of sales? "You get to eat what you kill." I think that it's up to us alone to do the things that are necessary to create our revenue in this business. It's not up to the customers to come to us; it's up to us to get the customers. It's not up to our competition to leave us alone; it's up to us to separate ourselves from the competition. If it's to be, it's up to me.

Change also means keeping up with progress and technology. It has been said that if a change on the outside of your company is occurring faster than the changes on the inside, then the end is in sight.

KEY POINTS: KERP

- Increase your **K**nowledge by tapping into **E**xperience, **R**esources, and a sound **P**hilosophy.
- Work on this every day.
- Ask existing clients why they do business with you; ask what they liked and what they didn't like.
- If you aren't training, you aren't gaining.
- Adopt a philosophy of total responsibility.
- Tap into the experience of those around you.
- Learn from your failures and those of others.
- Resources include customers, competitors, seminars, books, top salespeople, your peers, the Internet, tapes,and magazines.
- You need knowledge of your product, price, customers, and competition.
- You cannot expect your results to change unless you change.
- If change outside your company is occurring faster than change on the inside, the end is in sight.

GAME

We have a lot of work to do. We have to be very well prepared. We have to learn to play the GAME. It's a new GAME, and there are new rules. We're going to learn to play it better than our competitors do. Something to keep in mind is the fact that your competition might not be other companies selling the same product/service that you are. It  could be your prospect's landlord. It might be the phone company or any other bill that they've got to pay. It might even be their children's college tuition. So how do you make sure your prospects do business with you? How do you make sure that they entrust you with their money? You've got to learn to play the GAME: **G**oals, **A**ttitude, **M**echanics, **E**ffort.

• •
There is no such thing as time management without the exercise of goal setting.
• •

Goals

I can imagine you thinking, "Oh no, another guy talking about goals. I've seen the videos. I've read the books. I've listened to the tapes. Enough, already." But we need to discuss goals. Do you ever have problems with time management? Would you like to know how to be better with your time, how to get more out of your day? Now you're saying, "Wait a minute; you were talking about goals a second ago." There is no such thing as time management without the exercise of goal setting. Here's an exercise I learned from Stephen Covey:

I want you to imagine some-thing. You've got a gallon jar. I come along with a box of big rocks. I put these rocks inside the jar, filling it to the top. The jar's full, right? NO, because I pull out a bag of pebbles. I pour the pebbles over the big rocks so they tumble down into the  nooks and crannies and fill the jar to the top. Now the jar's full, isn't it? No. Now I've got a bag of sand. I pour the sand over the pebbles and the rocks. It goes all the way down into the cracks to fill that jar to the top, so that now it's *really* full. Yes? No. I've got a pitcher of beer now, and after I take a drink, I pour it over the sand, the pebbles, and the big rocks until I truly do fill that jar to the top. Would you be able to do that in the reverse order, beer, sand, pebbles, and finally rocks? This exercise tells us that if you don't put the big rocks in first, you'll never get them in. When you set your goals, visualize that jar.

There are only two things we work on in the course of a day. I know; you think I'm crazy. You've got calls and e-mails. You've got customers coming. You've got all kinds of…. No; two things: We work on PRIORITIES or we work on URGENCIES. That's it! Those big rocks represent your priorities. Urgencies are represented by everything else – the beer, the sand, the pebbles. You have to identify your big rocks. We often find ourselves working on the things that come in after we've sat down to work on our priorities … though, typically, they don't come in afterwards, they come in during. Do you work on to-do lists? Have you failed to get through your to-do list, your priorities, in a day? Do you know what came up? Pebbles, sand, beer … martinis.

Visualize where you are right now as a salesperson … the customers you call on, what your book of business looks like, your personal income, the way you live, the environment around you, your culture, the level of success that you feel you have attained. Now visualize where you want to be in six months. We're going to draw a map. We'll list the steps necessary to get there, and break it down by month, by week, and by day. Now write down three to five things that will be different in six months. Be very clear about your vision.

- How many more sales will you make each month?
- How many more calls will you make each day?
- How many more referrals will you get from existing clients?
- How will your business life be different?
- How will your personal life be different?
- What will you drive six months from now?

When you've had one of those great, successful days in business, and you go home in the evening, are you a better communicator with your significant other or your kids, or a worse one? When I come home after a rough day, I'm not as good a dad. I'm not as good a husband. I'm not as good a communicator. If I get the crap beat out of me while I'm on the road for a week or two, when I come home I don't feel successful. My kids feel that too. I owe it to myself to be successful, but, more importantly, I owe it to my family. To even feel successful, I have to go through the process of being very clear about the goals that I set for myself, no matter how small they might be, because repeated small successes grow into larger successes.

• •

Define success and chart it all the way back to the present. How do you have to change your daily activities to get where you want to go?

• •

Have you listed the income you want to be making six months from now? Typically, when I ask salespeople this question, they say, "Well, I'm tracking about $5,000 a month right now. I want to be at $8,000 in six months." Now break that down. How much do you make per sale? How many meetings does it take to close one deal? How many calls do you make to get one meeting? Define success and chart it all the way back to the present. Ask yourself how you have to change your daily activities to get where you want to go. Wanting to get there isn't going to do it. By *acting* to get there, you have a shot. By knowing clearly what you have to do, you will be able to act appropriately.

One of the most important things to remember about your goals is that if you don't write them down, they're just dreams, and (as my great mentor Jack Daly continues to remind me) dreams rarely come true. Goals that are written down often do. When you write down your goals there's something magical that happens in the transfer of ink to paper that creates more commitment. When it's written down it's almost a self-fulfilling prophecy. I know that sounds sort of metaphysical, but do it! If you don't write down your goals, they're just wants, wandering generalities: "I want to make more money. I want to be a professional football player. I want to drive a better car …."

Some people set goals, write them down, and then forget about them. Then at the end of the year they say, "That didn't work." I look for salespeople who say, "Damn it, I'm going to drive my stake into the ground and take what's mine because I have that opportunity as a salesperson." I want them to look in the mirror and say, "I feel sorry for the competition because I'm going to kick some serious butt today. There's nothing that's going to stop me from reaching my goals, the goals that I have committed to."

• •
Write down your goals and reach them once, and you'll absolutely change your life forever.
• •

Another key to achieving goals is not to make them ridiculously big or long-term: "I'm going to make a million dollars by the time I'm twenty-four." That's a wandering generality. What are you going to do in six months? Break down the activities that you have to do in those months and achieve small but steady successes. Let me tell you, all you have to do is write down your goals and reach them once, and you'll absolutely change your life forever.

Now look at the obstacles that might be in the way of achieving your goals. Some are real and some are perceived. Competition can be an obstacle. Your training, your knowledge, your skills, your experience or lack thereof, your staff, the size of your sales force, your customer base – these are all potential obstacles.

Many people believe that in building a sales force, we have to manage with a carrot or with a stick. They think that you either have to provide your salespeople with prizes they can reach for, or you have to get behind them and whup 'em until they get where you want them to be. I firmly believe that instead of pushing people into what I want for them, I must find out what *they* truly want. Then I can get in front of them and pull them toward their goals. They're going to let themselves down on their goals a lot quicker than I'm going to let them down on THEIR goals.

I've been talking about playing the game – getting in and playing the GAME to be more effective in the field of sales. Let's recap setting goals and what you need to do to achieve them.

- Be very clear on where you want to be, down to the smallest of details.
- Identify your "big rocks."
- Know what you have to do regularly to achieve your goals.

- Realize that you have to get rid of anything that's not a big rock. Of course, urgencies do come up, and you can't disregard all of them, but if you're not focused on your big rocks, then your natural inclination will likely be to focused on anything *but* your big rocks.

- Whatever your goals are – whatever you want to change or whatever you want to accomplish, wherever you want to go and however you want to get there – *write it down*. Get a goal book. Get a binder, a notebook, something that's yours. Write it down. If you want to dig even deeper, share your goals with somebody.

- When you write down goals, *commit* to achieving them.

- Regularly review your goals. Make sure you're tracking them. Define what success will be for you and then chart it back to the present.

My priorities are my children and my family. I also have business priorities: Delivering the right message for my customers and growing my business. And they're related. The better I achieve my business goals, the better I will be able to take care of my family. Yes, it does mean I have to do some things that are uncomfortable for me, things that require me to get outside my comfort zone. It means that I have to be on airplanes a lot. It means that I will have to miss some family events, and that I will have to pass up some business opportunities.

When my younger daughter had her first ballet recital, I had it marked in my calendar for about six months prior to the day. I turned down four speaking engagements for that date (each of which would have brought in about $15,000) because the recital was scheduled and it was a priority. Now, every ounce of my entrepreneurial being screamed in pain when I had to turn down business of that magnitude, but my daughter will never have a *first* ballet recital again in her life, and I'm so glad I was there. However, if I hadn't been focused on my priorities as a result of having it written down, I probably would have said, "Videotape it. I gotta go."

So where are your priorities? Your big rocks can be personal as well as business-related.

• •

Attitude is 100 percent of the game. It dictates everything else.

• •

Attitude

Attitude is 100 percent of the game – not 50 percent … 100 percent. Why is attitude important? Because attitude dictates everything else. It dictates your work ethic. It dictates the way you dress. It dictates the way you interact with customers. There are two things you should protect with your life in this world. One of them is your time, one of the most important factors in a sales professional's life.. The other is your attitude.

In the field of sales, you cannot have a more important tool than your attitude. You need your attitude to get you "up" because you are a professional "no" taker. You wade through a sea of negativity just to get to that one "yes." You bang on a lot of trees before you find one that will fall. You do things for a living that terrify other people. You pick up the phone and sell. You try to persuade people on a regular basis to do business with you. It takes a special attitude to do that.

Some of the elements that make a salesperson strong are confidence and credibility. One way we can ensure that we always have the level of confidence we want, the level of credibility our customers look for, is to constantly build our KERP – our knowledge, our experience, our resources, and our philosophy. We are all entrepreneurs as salespeople ... CEOs of our own territories! We all have a stake in the success of our sales efforts. We all build a book of business inside the business that employs us. We all need to treat our careers like they are our own companies, whether you work for someone else or whether it *is* your company. And that comes down to attitude. How are you going to be focused on it? Keep the fire in your belly burning. Hold on to the "I can, I will" attitude. You have a choice; choose to do these things.

Attitude makes you sit up, listen, and pay attention because it is your career. Attitude makes you *not* listen to negativity or to something that will hold you back. Do you have a little clique at your office that hangs out at the water cooler and talks that negative talk, the stinking thinking?

"Did you hear about this person?"
"Yeah. I hear we're not getting a 401(k)."
"So-and-so's doing this."
"So-and-so's doing that."

● ●
Look for gold nuggets and make them the next step in your career.
● ●

It's easy to fall into that pattern of negative thinking and get into the pity closet. It's easy to get mired down in a two-day sales meeting that you assume is going to waste your time. I'll give you a tip: Look for gold nuggets in that meeting. Out of ten hours, you might get fourteen minutes of value. Take those fourteen minutes and make them the next step in your career. You'll learn something. You just have to wade through the swamp to get there. You have to work to maintain a positive attitude.

We've all had days when our confidence was sky high, we stunk of success, and the sales were affected accordingly. We've also had days when we felt a little meager, rather than eager, when we felt that we didn't have it all together. Think about those days when you get up and the food just tastes better, you get the green lights, your favorite song's are on the radio, customers are taking your calls, setting appointments, and doing business with you. Things just seem to flow. What do you think came first, those results or your attitude? Were you in a good mood at home before you even left for work? What came first? Subconsciously, I bet you had a choice in the morning. But we tend to let our mood be affected by whatever happens in our day because that's easier than being proactive and making our day be affected by our mood. It's easier to get up on the negative side. So you have to make a choice when you get up: "I'm going to take what's mine today. I'm going to make a difference. I'm going to affect my volume today. I'm going to affect my customers' lives."

I feel personally rewarded as a trainer and a speaker not because I get to talk in front of people, but because the things I do will turn on a few lights in the minds of two or three people in any audience. They'll create new actions for themselves and new results, and they will generate entirely new income for themselves, and it will change the lives of their children. I can lay my head down at night knowing that I want to focus on my audience and make sure that I can move a few people to that level. So my attitude has to feed on that. Doing so makes me more effective than simply thinking, "I've got to put together another program and practice it again," because the details of how you get where you're going can sometimes be mundane.

● ●

Make three people feel a little bit better about themselves each day, and watch what happens to you.

● ●

One thing you can do to make your attitude better is to make someone else's attitude better. Make a conscious effort each day for the next thirty days to help three people get into better moods. Say to the waitress who serves you well, "Listen, I just want to thank you for the outstanding service you've given me today. You must make a good living working here, because you are excellent at what you do. Thanks again."

If you've got employees, when was the last time you said thank you to them when they made that little extra effort? Recognize somebody … thank somebody for a job well done. Let somebody in ahead of you when you're driving. Make three people feel a little bit better about themselves each day, and watch what happens to you. Watch how you'll change. Note that I'm not talking about customers. We all want to kiss up to the customers. I mean other people, random encounters that you have throughout the day. You interact with probably fifty to a hundred people in a day, so why not make at least three of them feel better? You cannot help but go home and feel better yourself. You get what you give.

People have asked me for years, "How do you make your attitude better? Isn't it something you either have or don't have?" No, it's not; it's a choice. Whenever there's a recession, I choose not to participate in it. I choose not to carry any kind of baggage around with me. Everybody's got personal problems, right? Everyone's got issues, challenges. Everybody's got economic and financial woes from time to time. You can choose to let those drag you down, or you can treat them as just another factor in your life. Again, it's a choice.

Mechanics

Mechanics is another word for skills. What skills are necessary for you to be effective in the profession of sales on a regular basis? Do you have to prospect for customers? *How* do you prospect? Do you want to grow your company by bringing on new customers? Would it be fair to say that relationship development skills are very important?

Define the skills that are necessary for you to be an effective salesperson. Where do you think you're lacking? Are you a good communicator? Do you freeze up when you're on the phone? When you meet with someone in person, are you OK once you get rolling, but you have a hard time getting started? That's one thing that I had to work on as a salesperson. Once I got five minutes into a meeting, I was fine. When I started working as a speaker, the first five or ten minutes of a lecture were excruciating for me. I would think, *What have I gotten myself into?* I would start slowly, but by the end I was unstoppable. I had to work on overcoming that the same way I had to work on it when I was a salesperson. The problem was that I wasn't as prepared as I needed to be. I had to carefully *plan* the first five minutes: *Here's what I'm going to cover. I'll find a few people in the audience, get their names, and help them to feel comfortable about me.* There was a fear factor in speaking, just as there had been in sales. I had to *practice* what I planned to say by performing it over and over. As Tony Robbins says, "Repetition is the Mother of skill!"

A missing skill like that could be one of the obstacles I was talking about earlier. You have to break through a barrier. What other skills might you need to work on? How are you on the phones? How are you with your follow up? Assess your toolbox.

· ·

If you make the same number of calls today that you made yesterday, you'll get the same results that you got yesterday. Work harder and work smarter.

· ·

Effort

Effort is activity. If you make the same number of calls today that you made yesterday, you'll get the same results that you got yesterday. If you want to do better, you need to do more. How do you expect your results to change if you're not willing to change first? So sharpen your ax. Take some actions that are a little different, a little bit outside the box. Effort – activity – comes down to doing the right things and doing them more often. Work harder and work smarter. Put your efforts into the goals that you have identified. Focus your activity on your big rocks.

KEY POINTS: GAME

- **G**oals, **A**ttitude, **M**echanics, **E**ffort
- Attitude + Skills + Activity = Success
- Set your goals: identify your "big rocks."
- Break down your goals and then write them down.
- Goals can be business-related or personal.
- Identify obstacles, real or perceived.
- Attitude is 100 percent of the game; you must work on it and maintain it.
- Attitude determines whether or not you listen to negativity.
- Look for gold nuggets.
- Guard your attitude with your life.
- Thinking you have a bad attitude becomes a self-fulfilling prophecy.
- Make three people feel better about themselves every day.
- Attitude is a choice.
- Define the skills necessary to be an effective salesperson.

- Make the same number of calls today that you made yesterday and you'll get the same results that you got yesterday.
- Activity comes down to doing the right things and doing them more often: Work harder *and* smarter.

• •

The shortest course on selling is four words: Ask questions and listen.

• •

THE SHORTEST COURSE ON SELLING

The shortest course on selling is four words: Ask questions and listen. That's a two-part course:

1. Ask Questions
2. and ... Listen.

God gave us two ears, and only one mouth, but we tend to focus on what we're going to *say*. We focus on how we're going to get our message across. We focus on how we're going to put our presentation together and how we're going to deliver our value proposition. (By the way, I say "value proposition" rather than "sales pitch" because people don't buy based on the cost of something – they buy based on the value it gives them through the benefits delivered in return for their investment.) I contend that if I'm going to sell to you, there must first be some communication between us. I don't know *how* to construct a value proposition for you until I know what you value. I don't know what your motivators are or what your pains, fears, and desires are. I don't know how you make buying decisions or what your buying style is. I don't know what your challenges are. When I ask questions and listen to your answers, you will tell me how to do business with you by telling me those things. You will tell me how to earn your business, but until then I'm just another self-centered sales guy with commission breath, pushing a product.

* *
The strongest sentences we can deliver to customers end in question marks. If we ask enough questions, our customers will tell us how to do business with them.
* *

Ask questions, then listen to the answers. I believe that the strongest sentences we can deliver to customers end in question marks. If we ask enough questions, every one of our customers will tell us how to do business with them.

* *
Never ask a question without a purpose.
* *

Here's an exercise you can try for one week. When you are calling on customers and prospects next week, go out of your way to ask ten more questions of everyone you talk to. Lawyers say you should never ask a question unless you know the answer. I say you should never ask a question without a purpose. Assume nothing; ask everything. Get a customer to sell *you* on *them* and what's important to them. They'll tell you how they need to hear the message that you want to deliver. Stop focusing on what you want to say and start focusing on the way your prospects need to hear it.

Let's say I'm selling an innovative software program to three accountants. It will help them organize their businesses so they can be more effective and productive. Would I sell to all three of them the same way, giving the same presentation, the same pitch? Would they all buy for the same reasons? The answer might be yes, but that's unlikely. One accountant may just need to get more organized. Maybe one of the other accountants has software already, but it is giving him problems and mine is a bit better. Maybe the third accountant just thinks, "Damn, this guy's good-looking. I've got to buy something from him." They're all going to buy for different reasons, and unless I'm a professional and find out what those reasons are – unless I uncover their motivators – I won't know what those reasons are.

• •

There are three main motivators in life: pains, fears, and desires.

• •

There are three main motivators in life: pains, fears, and desires – that's it. There are a million subcategories under each one, but those are the basics. People run away from pain and fear, and they run toward their goals or desires.

If I ask enough questions in the course of my pitch to you – my presentation, my meeting, my mutual interview, which is what I prefer to call it – I'm going to uncover some pains. And when I find out what they are, I'm going to make a value proposition that will cure those pains. I'm going to uncover fears and challenges, and I'm going to put together a proposition that will bring peace of mind to some of those fears. I'm going to find out where you, my prospect, want to be, what your desires and goals are. I'm going to wave a magic wand and ask, "If money were no object, where would you like to see your company in a year?" I want to get you into a place where you can tell me some of your goals, some of your desires. Then I'll ask, "What needs to happen? What do you need to get out of the way first?" Once I find out those things, I can put together a value proposition that will help cure your pains, bring peace of mind to your fears, and create a bridge from where you are to where you want to be. I'll show you how my product can help build that bridge.

No matter what your product is, it relates to one of those three motivators. Imagine that you sell security systems. Guess what? Nobody wants to buy a security system. What they want to buy is peace of mind. You have to sell on trust. You have to sell peace of mind. You have to sell safety. You sell based on people's fears, people's concerns. What's a set of pots and pans? It's something that helps build a bridge to your prospect's desire to cook like a gourmet. How do you know? You ask questions that uncover that information. Ask what is important to them.

● ●

Build a bridge that brings the customer from where they are over to the product.

● ●

Let's try to visualize the bridge that gets your client from where they are to where they want to be. Imagine that you, as a salesperson, are standing on the bank of a great river. Your client is on the other side of the river on the opposite bank. Most salespeople will stand on the bank and scream: "Let me tell you about my product!" They're yelling over the roaring water.

The prospect is on the other side, typically not the least bit interested.

But you attend a seminar or you read a sales book that explains that you have to build a bridge between you and your client. You ask questions and start putting together your value propositions. And then you start to build a bridge to the other side of the river. It's important to have that bridge because you have to communicate ideas, and you can't do that from opposite sides of a river. Most salespeople build the bridge starting on *their* side of the river.

DO YOU KNOW WHAT THE PROS DO? THEY JUMP IN THE WATER, SWIM TO THE OTHER SIDE, AND START ASKING THE CUSTOMERS WHAT'S IMPORTANT TO THEM. THEY BUILD A BRIDGE THAT BRINGS THE CUSTOMER *FROM WHERE THEY* ARE OVER TO THEIR PRODUCT OR SERVICE. That's professional sales. You tell me how you can do that with a pitch. Tell me how you can do that with a canned presentation. You can do that only with questions. If you want to sell more, open your customers by swimming to their side of the river.

•••••••••••••••••••••••••••••••••••••
Two reasons to ask questions are to build rapport and to gather intelligence.
•••••••••••••••••••••••••••••••••••••

Questions are your most powerful tool in a sales presentation. Imagine sitting down with a client who said, "You can ask me a hundred questions, anything you want to know about me, my business, or what's going on. I'll answer up to a hundred questions." That's a dream customer! Could you come up with a hundred questions? Try it. The first twenty-five will be easy. The next twenty-five will be a bit harder. You're really starting to dig for the next twenty-five. But the final twenty-five are going to be really important questions. Did you know that you can ask the same question two or three or four times? The first time you get the top-of-consciousness answer. The second time you get an answer that goes a little deeper. The third time you get to the true motivator. Then, you hear about the pain, the fear, or the desire.

There's another part to this assignment. Beside each of the one hundred questions you come up with, write its purpose. I believe there are six reasons to ask questions:

1. To build initial rapport, trust, and like-ability.
2. To get the "Lay of the Land" (Who they are, what they're doing today, who they are buying from, how they make their decisions, etc.)
3. To Discover Pains
4. To Discover Fears
5. To Discover Desires
6. To Create a Deficit

Have you read *Swim with the Sharks: Without Being Eaten Alive* by Harvey Mackay? This book contains the "Mackay 66," 66 individual points that account representatives working for the Mackay Envelope Corporation were required to find out about all of their prospects, customers, and clients. Going down the first page, you'll see that the questions aren't too bad. You've got marital status, wedding anniversary, things like that. Go a little further and you get into lifestyle. Does the customer drink? If yes, what and how much? If no, are they offended when other people drink? Does the customer smoke? If no, are they offended when other people do? What kind of spectator sports do they like? What are their favorite teams? What kind of cars are they into? The list goes even further, getting into moral and ethical considerations that are involved when you work with the client.

If you knew only 50 percent of these items about each of your customers, you couldn't help but have a stronger relationship, and by virtue of that, how could they do business with someone else? This isn't the kind of information that you get by saying, "Here, let me just leave this with you. Fill it out and fax it back to me." I guarantee that if you do this one exercise, and identify even just thirty to forty items that would be important to you in your business for each prospect and customer, you'll double your sales in a year. This is about asking questions. This is about listening to the answers. This is about finding out about them, and, quite frankly, in the process you can't help but share a bit of information about yourself. Think this is intrusive? I don't! In fact, I believe it shows the prospect or customer that you care. And, as Zig Ziglar says, "They don't care how much you know until they know how much you care!" Customers tend not to want to hurt their friends, so they'll continue to do business with you as long as you've earned that right.

··································

**The stronger your relationships with your
customer, the more you earn the right to
mess up every once in a while and not
lose their business.**

··································

Do you know what else will happen when you build this relationship? We make mistakes in business sometimes, don't we?
We get orders wrong occasionally. But the stronger your relationships with your customer, the more you earn the right to
mess up every once in a while and not lose their business as a
result. So you see, it's not just a matter of gaining the business
and keeping the business; it's also a matter of buying yourself
the right to make the inevitable mistake.

If you want to be a true sales professional, if you genuinely
want to grow your book of business, what more do you need to
find out about your customers? This doesn't have to be a daunt-
ing task. Identify your top five customers or clients. (Customers,
I believe, do business with us once; clients do business with us
on an ongoing basis and refer more business to us.) Make up
your personal list of thirty-five to forty points that you'd like to
find out about those five customers/clients, then set a deadline
for gathering that information. It's going to take some lunches.
You'll have to get together, possibly with their families. I'm
happy to sit down with my clients and talk, or to drop by their
businesses. If a client is working late and struggling with something, I can give a couple hours of my time to demonstrate that
I'm not like everybody else, which says, "I'm here, and I'm
focused on getting something done for you."

Shut up and sell!

We were taught to get out there and get deals. If at the end of my presentation, my value proposition, I haven't done a good job, then we shouldn't do business together. If I have, we'll figure out some way to get it done because you won't want to do business with anybody else. We've started a relationship. Here's something I love to say in seminars: "Shut up and sell! Shut up and sell something, will you?" They'll tell you everything you need to know. It comes down to focusing on the customer, not on closing a deal.

KEY POINTS: SHORTEST COURSE ON SELLING

- Ask questions and listen.
- Your customers will tell you how to earn their business.
- Don't ask a question without a purpose.
- Assume nothing. Ask everything.
- There are three motivators in life: pains, fears, and desires. Identify those of your customers.
- Make value propositions that cure their pains, offer peace of mind for their fears, and create bridges to their desires.
- Ask the same question several times.
- Build a relationship; it buys you the right to make a mistake.
- Find out how your client has made decisions in the past.
- Identify your top five clients and list thirty-five or forty points that you'd like to find out about them.
- Shut up and sell!

● ●

You can't *find* time; you can't *make* time.
Time is there. The only thing you can do
is to schedule it.

● ●

YOU CANNOT MANAGE TIME

Many people say they have problems with time management. Well, there's bad news with that. You see…you cannot manage time. You can only manage yourself and your activity within the time that is available. The only thing that you can manage is the sequence of events during the time that you have. So if you think that you have to manage time better, realize that you can't; there is no such thing as time management. You have the same amount of time as everyone else. You can manage only what you do with that time. Have you ever said, "I just can't seem to find the time to get that done" or "I need to make the time to return that phone call"? More bad news: I have personally hired some of the world's top chemists and physicists to see if they could make more time … couldn't get it done! I even went so far as to hire the world's top archeologists and explorers to see if they could FIND more time … NO LUCK! You can't *find* time; you can't *make* time. Time is there. The only thing you can do with time is to schedule it.

Do you prospect in your business to get more customers? Here's a tip: SCHEDULE the time for prospecting every day, just as if it were a sales appointment, and hold that "appointment" more sacred than you do a sales meeting. Here's why: In that two or three hours, you might call thirty or forty companies. You have the opportunity to set possibly three or four or five appointments. Those appointments might turn into a couple of sales for you. What does one sales appointment turn into? At most, one sale.

If you have to eat a whole bunch of frogs, eat the biggest one first. Get the hardest things out of the way first.

I'm not saying you should disregard your sales appointments – that's the whole purpose of prospecting – but don't drag that 200-pound phone to your ear and then say, "Oh, somebody's here; I've got to see them." "Incoming call…I'm on it!" Schedule the time you need to get things done, especially the tasks that you don't particularly want to do. We all know there are certain things with which we're not that comfortable that we have to do everyday, but, as Brian Tracy says, "If you have to eat a frog, don't stare at it too long. If you have to eat a whole bunch of frogs, go ahead and eat the biggest one first." Every day we have to do tasks that are not necessarily the things we want to do. Get the hardest things out of the way first. Have you ever had to call a customer with bad news?

> … "Your ad didn't get placed the way you wanted it."
>
> … "You missed this issue."
>
> … "Your order didn't make the truck."
>
> … "The alarm system is coming in $400 more than we thought it would."

We tend to put those calls off. But two weeks later your customer's still calling you.

You're thinking, *Yeah, that voice mail – that's the third time he's called. I've got to get back to him. I'll just check my e-mail first....* DON'T! Tackle that call.

Identify your priorities based on your objectives, your big rocks, and work smarter and harder than ever before to achieve them if you want to be more effective. It's better to pave the road in advance rather than to navigate the potholes when we get to them. Our axes have to be sharper. We have to do IT more and we have to do IT better, whatever *IT* is. If you've made twenty calls a day for the past few years, you had better ramp yourself up to forty. But (and this is important), make sure it is the *right* forty, done the *right* way!

Wasting time can mean professional suicide. The best two ways to use your time are:
1. prospecting for new opportunities
2. serving existing clients

KEY POINTS: YOU CANNOT MANAGE TIME

- You cannot manage, find, or make time.
- The only things you can do are to schedule your time and to manage yourself and your activities within the available time.
- Wasting time can mean professional suicide.
- Schedule time for prospecting every day, just like it's a sales appointment.
- Get the hardest task out of the way first.
- Identify your priorities based on your objectives.

PREPARATION IS KEY

Have you gone on a vacation lately? You likely did some planning. You decided where you wanted to go and when, you chose accommodations, you booked some activities. Have you ever thrown a party? You probably planned that too. You made an invitation list and had the food planned. You may even have drawn maps so people could find the place. But do we do that degree of planning at work? We have to apply that level of planning in our careers. I'm sure you do some planning already – you've got appointments set up for next week, you've started to schedule your days, you know you're going to do some prospecting, and you know whom you're going to call.

● ●
Success can't be left to chance.
Success can be achieved only by design.
● ●

Success can't be left to chance. Success can be achieved only by design. You not only have to know whom you're going to call but also the *purpose* of those calls. You have to know what you want to take away from each meeting. If you don't close the deal, you need to know what you've gained, because if you don't close the deal, you had better have at least OPENED your prospect for the next opportunity. You have to know what you are looking for.

Now take the next step and practice your craft. Have you ever sat down in front of a mirror and practiced? Have you ever tape-recorded yourself prospecting? There's a stomach-churning little exercise for you if ever there was one. It can be a real eye-opener. Plan everything, and then practice it.

If, God forbid, you had a problem with your heart and required surgery, you'd probably assume that the cardiologist is up on his KERP – his knowledge, experience, resources, and philosophy. You would trust that he is a professional in the field of medicine and assume that he has the necessary tools and up-to-date manuals. It's probably safe to assume that you would not be the first person on whom he's operated…that maybe he's practiced this routine before. You'd also probably expect that he would plan the operation, that he would have all the right equipment there, and that the people who would be helping him would have done so before. You wouldn't expect to hear, "Anybody see where that scalpel went?" or, "Oh, damn. She's in cardiac arrest – what do we do now? Where are those jumpy things? Anybody got those?" You would expect a high degree of planning and practice because he's a professional in the field of medicine.

Do you deem yourself a professional in the field of sales? What do you think your customers expect of you? If I presented a seminar, and I fumbled with my notes and didn't necessarily know what I was going to say, you wouldn't think that I was a professional. But I've tapped into quite a bit of knowledge, experience, and resources and have the right philosophy to be successful as a speaker. Do you think that I preplan my presentations? Do you think I practice them? I've got two kids at home saying, "Ask questions, then listen!" I say to my wife, "Hey, honey, I've got a presentation tomorrow. Do you want to sit through this?" They've all sat through my presentations. I've got to plan and practice; my audience – my customers – DEMAND that from me! Your customers DEMAND it of you. If you don't do a good job, they won't buy from you. This is a blinding flash of the obvious. Be more prepared: plan and practice.

Customers throw out nasty little things called objections. Are you prepared to answer every one?

There are certain elements of a sales presentation that you can plan in advance. Customers ask questions. Are you prepared to answer just about every one? Customers throw out nasty little things called objections. Are you prepared to answer every one that comes up? Have you thought them out in advance? Have you thought, *This might come up. Here's how I might address it*? Have you written down your answers?

You can develop an objection guide. How many objections do you hear on a day-to-day basis? Six? Eight? Probably no more than ten. I've had people tell me that they encounter "millions" of objectives. When that happens, we sit down and try to list them. I've yet to come up with more than ten. What might the first one be? "The price is too high," or "I don't have the money today." How do you overcome that? Write the answer down. Tap into some experience. For every possible objection, ask every other salesperson in your organization how they would overcome that. I do this at seminars. We go all the way around the room, and by the time we get to the last salesperson in the corner, he or she has an answer that's unbelievable; it's coming out smooth and it covers everything. Why? Two reasons: He tapped into the experience of everybody who spoke before him, and he had time to prepare.

Here's another exercise. Take those objections and their answers and get together with two colleagues for fifteen minutes every day while you're having lunch. One of you wears the salesperson's hat, one is a customer, and the other observes. The customer gives the objection to the salesperson who reads back the answer. Go through each objection. Now switch places and go through them again. Go through them three times until each person has played each role. When you are the observer, take notes on what you liked and didn't like about what the others did and suggest any improvements.

That exercise is something I've done with companies and sales forces that I've run. And I've had some top-selling sales forces because I don't just schedule training; as the manager, training *is* my schedule. I have to figure out ways to get these people ramped up and making more money than they've ever made in their lives, and having more fun and working harder and smarter. But if I just teach them the words to say and send them out there, I'm not doing any better than if I were to say, "Here's a book about skating. Now go get in there, Wayne Gretzky!" That just wouldn't work; we have to practice.

You wouldn't say to your kids, "All right, kids. Let's sit around a conference table for a couple weeks; I'm going to teach you to swim"… and then at the end of two weeks just throw them into the deep end of the pool. They have to practice, and so do you if you want to learn and improve. We have to make our careers work more by design than by chance.

So why practice? It's only your career. You don't have to do it; it's only your career. It's only where you spend 50-60 percent of your waking hours. It's only the thing that, because of your success, feeds the rest of your life. It's only what pays your bills, feeds your children, puts clothes on your back and a roof over your head. You don't have to practice. You might think that you know what you're going to say, that you know your pitch, but have you ever had a customer throw you a curve ball? Have you ever had a customer say, while taking off his watch and putting it on the desk before you, "Stop. You asked for twenty minutes. You got twenty minutes. Now go"?

Were you thinking, *Oh, man. That's what I said on the phone, but I really need an hour*? Are you prepared for that? Have you practiced the twenty-minute drill? Have you practiced what you might say to get more time?

Have you practiced what to say when, after twenty minutes, the customer says, "Time's up, but I'm interested. See me next month"? These things come up, don't they? What about this one: "I've got four guys sitting in the lobby who sell the same thing you do, and you're price is 20 percent higher. Why should I buy from you?" Are you prepared to answer that question *before* it's asked? This whole book is really about preparation. How are you going to do it?

● ●
**A sales presentation is not a spectator sport.
It is a participatory sport.**
● ●

After preparation comes presentation. Here's what *not* to do: Don't go out and tell. Don't go out and say, "Let me tell you, let me tell you." YOU'VE GOT TO TRANSFER TRUST. Don't talk about your product, or talk about you. I've got to trust you. I've got to know that you're going to be committed to me as a customer. If I don't get those feelings, then I'm not doing business with you. When you present, you're going onstage just like an actor. The best actors get paid the most, just like in sales. Go out and perform. Go out and ask questions and listen. A sales presentation is not a spectator sport. It is a participatory sport. Listen, listen, listen. If the customer's talking more than you are during a sales presentation, that's a good thing. Instead of being interesting, try being interested! You'll be amazed at what happens.

KEY POINTS: PREPARATION IS KEY

- Plan your work.
- Practice it.
- Be prepared to answer your customers' objections; write your answers down.
- Don't go out and tell; go out and perform.

PROSPECTING, SEEING CUSTOMERS, AND FOLLOWING UP

Ask yourself, "Would *I* do business with me?" If all you say is, "Yes," what does that really tell you? You need to know why. How are you different? Do you sound better? Do you represent your industry better? How do you ensure that your clients do business with *you*? Have you ever walked out of a sales meeting feeling that the customer's going to buy from you, then nothing happens? "I chased it for three months, four months; she's not returning my calls anymore." How do you ensure that prospects think of you first when it's time to do business? How do you make sure that you are at the top of their consciousness? The time for passive selling is over. We have to be proactive.

• •

There are just three things that we should be doing every day. We do what's necessary to get in front of prospects, we are in front of them, or we're following up.

• •

MOTIVATION
MOTIV-ACTION

All motivation is – is the motive to take action. Once you're very clear on where you want to be six months from now – on what that vision is – then you identify your priorities to get you there. Those are your motives.

Now plan your actions. I believe that for salespeople, there are just three things that we should be doing every day.

1. We do what's necessary to get in front of prospects.

2. We are in front of them.

3. We're following up.

Those three things involve taking calls and MAKING calls. That's it! Non-selling activities are the absolute death of a salesperson.

Do you find yourself mired in non-selling activities daily? Filing, or reading and sending e-mails? The Internet's a big non-selling activity, but it's not going to go away. What you choose to do with it is up to you. E-mails are not going to stop coming into your mailbox. You have to manage your time so you can get things done. It's an issue of goal setting.

I've just said there are three critical tasks for sales professionals: prospecting, seeing customers, and following up. That's the simplest way to put it. Those are the "big rocks" of your work. Those have to go into the jar first.

Prospecting

Our first job is to do what's necessary to get in front of more customers, to create an opportunity to sell. This is appointment setting, prospecting, cold calling – or proactive calling for customer service people. Every call you make to an existing client is an opportunity to sell. It's an opportunity to serve. It's an opportunity to generate revenue. If it's not cash revenue, it's the revenue of trust, the revenue of belief. When your customers think, *This customer service person cares about me. My business is in their best interest; I will continue to give them business, refer them business, and grow their business because they are helping me grow mine* – that's revenue.

• •

You can get whatever you want in this life if you help enough people get what they want.

• •

Zig Ziglar has said, "You can get whatever you want in this life if you help enough people get what they want." I think it's just a matter of focus, especially in sales, so identify those big rocks.

There's nobody who loathes the phone more than I did when I was selling on a regular basis. But I knew that it was a necessary evil. I had two choices: I could call prospects on the phone or I could go out and knock on doors. Of course, there are lots of other ways to prospect; there's networking and touch campaigns and approach campaigns and so on, but the telephone was the most efficient use of TIME. So I figured that if I had to do it, then I had to learn to be the best.

Now, I knew the things that would interrupt me every day—the pebbles, the sand, the beer, especially the beer. I knew that as soon as someone approached me in my office, the interruption would take me out of my "zone." I had to get into a proactive outbound-calling mode, so I put on a ball cap. My rules were pinned up outside my cubicle:

- When my ball cap is on, I don't take calls.
- When my ball cap is on, don't come and talk to me.
- These are my prospecting times.
- This is when I'll be finished; I'll return calls then.

When the ball cap was on, calls were outbound only. I had to fool myself that much. I had to take those steps because I knew that I'd get sidetracked by anything, using any excuse not to dial that phone.

Guess what? IT WORKED!

There's a simple question that you need to ask yourself about every interaction with a prospect, every time you pick up the phone to set up an appointment, every time you meet with someone, every time you talk to your employees, every time you talk to your boss, and every time you talk to your spouse, for that matter. Ask this question: "What is the purpose of this call? What am I trying to accomplish?"

. . . .

If I try to explain my product on the phone it's like trying to get a haircut over the phone. We both end up looking silly.

. . . .

When you're prospecting, you're calling to set appointments. What's the purpose of that call? To sell something? No! You are trying to set an appointment. That's it. I'm very clear about the purpose of my calls when I'm prospecting. I don't have to give my prospects a ton of information. I don't have to dazzle them or tell them how long we've been in business and how we differ and so on. Yes, I want an opportunity to tell them that, but if I try to explain it on the phone it's like trying to get a haircut over the phone. We both end up looking silly. The purpose of my call is to book fifteen minutes of their time. We'll know within the first five whether we have a match or not, and if not, quite frankly, I'll get out of your hair. But if it does look like we have a match, then I'm prepared to make you my value proposition.

What's the purpose of leaving a voice mail message, by the way? TO GET A RETURN CALL! That's all. Why is it that we ramble on so much when we leave messages?

What's the purpose of the first sales appointment? To establish a relationship! Nine out of ten people will tell you that a meeting is to get the business, to close the deal – and that's the way they come across. When I meet with my prospects, I want to find out about them, their pains, fears, and desires, and I want to transfer trust. Until I do that I can't worry about making a sale. Sometimes salespeople make general proactive calls. They call all their customers each week just to "touch base" or to see how things are going. Don't. Never make a call without a clear purpose. Have something to offer, something to say. Have a question or two (or ten) to ask. If you know going in what the purpose of the contact is, it takes you a step closer to your goals.

Expand this concept: What's the purpose of your day? If you're prospecting, what's the purpose of that whole exercise? It doesn't matter if you can make twenty calls, thirty calls, or fifty – the point of the exercise is to set five appointments, to get five opportunities to generate revenue for your family. The purpose is not to go through the calls that your sales manager wants you to make just so you can post your numbers and make your manager happy.

● ●
Success in prospecting is directly tied to your mental outlook.
● ●

Here are some key prospecting tips:

- GET YOUR HEAD AND HEART INTO THE GAME! Your success in prospecting is directly tied to your mental outlook. If you loathe prospecting and see it as just a necessary evil, guess how you're going to sound on the phone? "I hate this. My manager told me to make forty calls today. You don't want to buy anything from me, do you? OK, goodbye." That's the way it will comes across. Your attitude toward prospecting is so important. Make sure you're in the right frame of mind before you pick up that phone. After all, it's only your career.

- GET ORGANIZED! Every lost or forgotten lead, every missed opportunity, is devastating. You know how it happens: You're at a Chamber of Commerce event, you have a couple of drinks, you meet someone who says, "Call me; I'm interested possibly." Now, what did you do with that business card? Here's another organizational tip: Set up your whole day. Set up your meetings and appointments. Schedule your prospecting time. If you're making proactive calls or prospecting, you're setting up your success when you set up that time. Don't do things by chance. Organize your desk. Log information in your database. Do whatever is necessary.

- DO *IT* MORE, but don't run up blind alleys. Make sure your activity is high quality and high quantity.

- RECOGNIZE ALL QUALITY LEADS and opportunities more quickly. Your competition isn't sitting around, so you can't either. If you really want to do better, imagine that your main competitor is the best salesperson in the world and that they've got all the latest technology. They've got a pipeline full of leads. If they even sniffed at your customers, your customers would be interested, and then your competitor would be all over them like a cheap suit. Act quickly!

- LOOK FOR LEADS EVERYWHERE! The phone is only one way to prospect. Use as many ways as you can.

> ●
> ## If you're not getting referrals,
> ## either you're not asking for them or
> ## you don't deserve them.
> ●

- LOOK FOR MORE REFERRALS AND REPEAT BUSI-
  NESS. Vertically integrate into all existing clients. It is crucial
  to vertically penetrate your market, getting more business
  through existing customers. You can do this directly from
  them or through their networks of clients, referrals, strategic
  alliances, and so on. If you're not getting referrals from your
  existing customers right now, you're missing an opportunity. If you want referrals, ask. Asking is half the getting. If
  you're not getting referrals, either you're not asking for them
  or you don't deserve them. Whichever it
  is, you need to change something. Make
  it easy for your clients to refer to
  you. Give them a reason to do so.
  Everybody's tuned into that old radio station, WII-FM, What's In It For
  Me? Find something in it for them,
  whether it's a discount on their next
  purchase or just a thank you.

- AGAIN, DO IT MORE! Don't strategize about how you're
  going to do it, just do it. Call more and call better.

- PERSONALIZE EVERYTHING. This is called branding.
  Get your name on everything; name recognition is very important. Personalize everything as a sales professional, all
  your cards, e-mails, letters, voice mails, notes, and faxes –
  everything has to be different from your competitors'. I

change my voice mail greeting four or five times per week. Each time I give a different quote. If a prospect calls and they don't get me because I'm at a speaking engagement or something like that, then I want them to hear something that gives them a feeling for who I am. That is part of building a positive perception of difference for myself. How will you differentiate yourself on your pager, your cell phone, or your home voice mail?

- REMEMBER THAT PURPOSE LEADS TO FOCUS; focus precedes success.

● ●
Hold your prospecting time sacred.
● ●

- HOLD YOUR PROSPECTING TIME SACRED. Schedule time for it every day and ensure that there are as few interruptions as possible.

- DO YOUR HOMEWORK. Before you contact your prospect, have a clue, have a plan. Don't go in half-cocked. Think about everything you need to know. Know what their business is about. Know what the competition is. Do some research. Find out something that might be common ground, something that might spark their interest when you call and give them a reason to want to take it further. Gathering information also ensures that you're not just running around collecting as many leads as possible. Make sure they are the leads you want. Identify your ideal customers. To do that, you've got to do your homework. You've got to read the periodicals, read the newspapers. Project the lifetime value of your prospects and what you have to do to go after those prospects.

- REMEMBER THAT CONSISTENCY IS CRUCIAL. Anyone can get fired up and do what's necessary for success for the next week or two. It's how you keep it going that's important. How consistent is your attitude? How consistent are your skills, your activity, and your efforts? How consistent is your prospecting? How consistent are the networking events you attend? How consistent are the cards you send out? Do you send them systematically or just when you feel like it? How about the e-mails you send? How consistent are you when prospects and clients call in? Do they know they're going to talk to someone with an upbeat attitude every time?

• •

It costs six times more to find a new client than it does to get an existing one back.

• •

Seeing Customers and Following Up

Remember, there are three things salespeople should be doing. The first one is prospecting, *getting* in front of customers. Number two and number three, *being* in front of customers and following up, are related. These two consist of making value propositions, giving sales presentations, building rapport, and developing and maintaining relationships. It costs six times more to find a new client than it does to get an existing one back. That means we must take the time to cultivate our existing clients.

How often are you "in front of" your prospects and clients with a postcard, an e-mail, a fax, a lunch, or something else that separates you from the competition? As a sales professional, you're chopping down trees, right? You might get halfway through a tree, it might start to teeter, and then suddenly it becomes solid as a rock. You know that eventually something will knock that tree down, but you might walk away and start looking for other trees, thinking you'll get back to that tree later. Maybe next year…. But there's a tree that's halfway chopped down! Don't abandon it. Keep working on it. Keep in touch.

You started the sale process on that tree, that prospect. You set an appointment. That's a major win, isn't it? How many calls did you make to set one appointment? This prospect didn't tell you to get out – another win. He didn't say he wasn't interested. He said you should call him back after the first of the year. What do 99 percent of salespeople do when they hear that? They call back after the first of the year.

* *
We're not order takers; we're order *makers*.
* *

But we're not order takers; we're order *makers*. He said *call* him after the first of the year. That doesn't mean you can't send him a handwritten note saying, "Thank you so much for allowing me to share my enthusiasm over our product with you. Really looking forward to doing business with you at the beginning of the year. Should your needs change between now and then, please make sure that you consider me." That's the handwritten note he's going to get from me, or he's going to get a fax from me. I'm going to scour some articles and some business periodicals that relate to his business. I'm going to read the newspapers.

I subscribe to about thirty magazines. I can't sit down and read thirty magazines in a month, but I fly about thirty thousand miles a month too. I carry a big backpack full of magazines, and I go through them on the plane. If a headline looks good, I rip the story out and stick it in a file. When I leave, I have a file containing just what's important. I'm looking for items that might be interesting or important to me, but I also think about my clients and the people I've been involved with professionally. I look for articles that might be of interest to them. I send these clippings out with little notes: "Still thinking about you. Hope you're doing the same. Thought you might enjoy this." What are the chances that my competitors are doing that?

If you're one of my prospects and you get that from me, you're going to think, *Wow, here's this guy again. Now I remember him. And he's remembering me. He's thinking about me. He's not on to the next deal. He's not whacking away at some other tree; he's still chipping at this one.* That's the most important part.

Those are the actions that separate you from the rest of the field, from your competitors. Figure out some way to keep in touch with your prospects and clients. Again, this is important because it's not whom you know; it's who knows *you*. Have you ever gone back to a prospect after several months for another meeting, and the prospect says, "What's your name again? And this was about what?" We want them to say, "I'm so glad you came back in. You know, those clippings you sent me were great."

● ●

Three words can differentiate you from your competitors: thank you notes.

● ●

Three words can differentiate you from most of your competitors: thank you notes. How many have you written this week? Do you send personal, handwritten notes thanking your prospects for their time? Do you do so whether they say yes or whether they say no? Do it by design, not by chance. If somebody throws you out, send her a note thanking her for allowing you to get on to your next appointment more quickly.

I have to be different from my competitors because maybe I'm not better. Maybe I'm not as sharp or as smooth a talker, so I have to do things differently. I have to create a better perception … make a stronger impact! Look at your mechanics, your skills. Figure out what you need to do to create that positive perception of difference in your customers' minds, such that they will go out of their way and/or pay a premium to do business with you. If you're my client and you're on my mailing list, every two months you'll get a postcard for some event, with a picture of my partner and me on the front of it. Many people get Christmas cards; my clients got Thanksgiving cards one year. It was just a goofy little card with a picture of me dressed as an Indian and my partner dressed as a Pilgrim, with our thumbs up. It said, "Thumbs up this Thanksgiving," and on the back it said, "When you're thinking about growing your business, hire eagles and have the turkeys for Thanksgiving." It was a quick touch piece.

The only way to be sure that your customers think of you first is through frequent, repetitious contact.

Stay in constant touch with active prospects through phone calls, periodic mailings, e-mails, and other personal contacts. This type of touch campaign uses the top-of-consciousness principle, which states that the only way to be sure that your customers think of you first is through frequent, repetitious contact. It doesn't have to be expensive, but don't just make it phone calls or just e-mails. It can't be just cards or letters. The competition is always vying for your prospects' and customers' attention – and their dollars.

Let's say your prospect is not ready to buy. Your prospect is that tree, halfway cut through, that you abandoned. You never know when that prospect's motivation to buy will suddenly and dramatically increase. You don't know when that tree's going to fall. If you've forgotten them – if you aren't in front of them somehow with a card, a fax, an e-mail, a phone call, lunch, a golf game, something – even if they're not buying today, what happens when that changes? How do you make sure they call *you*? That's an opportunity, and the one who makes the sale is simply the one who capitalizes on that opportunity the best. You need to be sure that your prospects think of you and your company first when they evaluate how to fulfill their business needs.

KEY POINTS: PROSPECTING, SEEING CUSTOMERS, AND FOLLOWING UP

- There are only three things you should be doing: Getting yourself in front of customers (prospecting), being in front of them (seeing customers), or following up.
- Know the purpose of each call, mailing, e-mail, meeting, event, question.
- Prospecting tips:
  - proper attitude is essential: have fun
  - organizational skills are essential
  - more activity is required
  - recognize all quality leads and opportunities more quickly
  - look for leads everywhere
  - look for more referrals and repeat business
  - double your prospecting time
  - personalize everything
  - purpose leads to focus; focus precedes success
  - hold your prospecting time sacred
  - do your homework: before you contact your prospect, have a plan (know what their business is about, know what the competition is, etc.)
  - consistency is crucial
- It costs six times more to find a new client than it does to keep an existing one.
- Figure out ways to stay in constant touch with your prospects and customers – you never know when they'll decide to buy.
- It's not who you know; it's who knows you.
- Three words can differentiate you from most of your competitors: thank you notes.
- Follow up.

•••••••••••••••••••••••••••••••••
I don't believe it's who you know that matters; it's who knows *you*.
•••••••••••••••••••••••••••••••••

BUILDING YOUR (P.P.O.D.)
POSITIVE PERCEPTION OF DIFFERENCE: YOUR SPECIAL SAUCE

What perception of difference do you create in the marketplace such that people will go out of their way or pay a premium to do business with you – or both? How do you get outside the box? How do you sound different from every person who comes through the door? How do you come across differently? Not just in what you say and how you say it – that's not enough. You also must have the ACTIONS with which to back up your words. How often do you get in touch with the customer?

What counts is how you treat those you know. The rules have changed, and we have to work harder and smarter to keep up.

How do you differentiate your product? Is it with your presentation? Do you use a PowerPoint presentation? Do you use flip charts? Graphs? Do you use different marketing materials? Do you flip through presentation books? Do you even know what the real presentation is, what your true product is? Every one of your customers, whether they say this out loud or not, is thinking, *Why should I do business with you?* Not your company – that doesn't matter; we're not there yet. Why should they do business with *you*? How do you answer that question?

There are things you can say – you're honest, you're hardworking, you're trustworthy – and they could be and should be true. But those words put you in the same boat as the next person and the next person and the next. They say those things too. What do you *do* that answers that question? What do you do before you make the call, and what do you do afterward, that separates you from the rest? If you prospect on the phone, how do you sound different from the last ten people who called? I'm not talking just about competitors in your industry, but the last ten people who called to take some of your prospect's time. Every person vying for the dollar of that client is a competitor. So how do *you* sound different, walk differently, talk differently, act differently? You could put together different marketing materials, but those materials are going to be scrap paper unless you OPEN your prospect first. If you make that initial IMPACT, then you've got a shot at discussing your product.

The second question that prospects and clients ask, if you get past the first one, is, "Why should I do business with your company?" Now we can get into our value propositions and our presentations. (Make sure they are tied to benefits!) And customers buy based on perception of value.

I believe you should answer both those questions – Why should I buy from you, and why should I buy from your company? – with questions.

• •
**You have to sweat everything,
right down to the smallest details.**
• •

Have you seen that book called *Don't Sweat the Small Stuff*? I don't agree. I think that you have to sweat everything, right down to the smallest details. Here's an example: The way your phones are answered. If I called your company today, would I get an automated attendant? Would I get an answering machine? Would I hear, "Mumble-hold-please"? I don't even know if I've got the right company if I hear that. We tend not to focus on our telephone receptionists, but I think the way your phones are answered is critical.

Is there a chance that someone has called your organization and been sent into voice mail hell, the black hole of the telephone world, where they must go through the corporate structure, pushing buttons? Or did they end up with an answering machine? Maybe they hung up and called the next name listed in the phone book after your phone rang five times. Those are lost opportunities. They say that in sales, sometimes half of success is just showing up…half of it's just picking up the phone. Make sure that happens.

Is it possible that the way your phone is answered – or not answered – has blown an opportunity for a sale? Sweat the small stuff: The way you walk, the way you talk, the way you act, the way you dress, the way you communicate.

Do you use e-mail now for communicating regularly with your clients? Do you think you use e-mail too much? How many e-mails do you get, thirty or forty a day? What's your favorite button, Read or Delete? Delete. Do you know why salespeople like to communicate via e-mail? It's easy! Because a lot of prospects and clients say the best way to contact them is by e-mail. But do you know what I hear when my clients say that? *One* way to contact them is with e-mail, but it's not my favorite way because there's no interaction. I don't even like the phone that much. I had to learn to be good on the phone for prospecting because it's necessary, but I want the enthusiasm, the eye contact, the smile, the give and take.

● ●
E-mail is just a tool, a tool that's becoming a crutch for many people.
● ●

You've got to focus on your clients and their needs. You have to show them that and you have to communicate that. E-mail is just a tool, a tool that's becoming a crutch for many people. When I talk to salespeople at the companies that I coach, I often ask how many customers they've contacted that day. Sometimes they say, "Every single one of them."

"No kidding? It's only 10:00 in the morning."
"Well, I sent out an e-mail blast."
"We need to talk."

In this high-tech world, being "high touch" separates us from the rest.

Have you ever arrived at a sales appointment five minutes late and figured it was just a little thing, no big deal? I'm guilty of that too. Always call if you're going to be late. Just showing up on time is half the battle sometimes, because if you're late, you're already starting in the hole. What you are telling the prospect when you arrive late is that you don't value their time. If you don't value their time as a prospect, how are you going to treat them once they've become clients?

What perception of value do you create that will cause people to go out of their way or pay more to do business with you?

It all comes down to this: What perception of value do you create that will cause people to go out of their way or pay more to do business with you? People do not buy based on reality the first time they buy from you – they buy based on the perception that you and your products are going to perform. Sell yourself and your uniqueness first. Then put together a solid value proposition based on the questions you've asked and the prospect's answers, and craft the presentation to suit their needs. As long as you do that, price doesn't matter.

How do you make sure that your customers do business with nobody *but* you? That takes relationship development. I don't know of anything more important in sales than relationship development. It costs six times more to get a new customer than it does to keep an existing one. There are different levels of salespeople out there – some who flip over a rock, get the deal, turn the customer over to customer service, and then move on to the next rock to get the next deal. Then there are sales professionals who are account managers. They flip over the rock, open the prospect, do a value proposition, make a proposal, close the initial deal, and then work to manage that account and serve that client. Which are you? For those of us in the customer service industry who are touching clients and working with them on a daily basis, those relationship development skills are paramount.

KEY POINTS: POSITIVE PERCEPTION OF DIFFERENCE

- People buy based on perception of value.
- How do you sound different on the phone than the last ten salespeople who called?
- Sweat everything, down to the smallest detail, such as answering the phone.
- In this high-tech world, being more "high touch" separates us from the competition.
- Be on time; if you show up even a little late you're already starting in the hole.
- As long as you're in the game with selling yourself and your company, price doesn't matter.
- Relationships are key.

Gerry Layo's Top 20 Tips
"THE LAYO 20"

1. Be the most positive and enthusiastic person you know.
2. Start each day the night before.
3. Get up early.
4. Read at least one book every month. (On sales, communication, negotiation, etc.)
5. Schedule your prospecting time (no less than one hour per day).
6. Schedule your e-mail/Internet time (no more than one hour per day).
7. Look sharper than everyone else.
8. Be on time, every time.
9. Be over prepared.
10. Make five people feel better about themselves every day.
11. Say thank you – a lot.
12. Ask questions, tons of questions; be curious, interested, and present during the answers.
13. No matter what or where your office may be – your office, your home, your hotel room, your car, your briefcase – keep it clean and organized, as if the world's greatest customer is about to walk in.
14. Guard two things with your life: your time and your attitude.
15. Avoid negative and pessimistic people.
16. Review your written goals every month.
17. Listen, listen, listen.
18. Schedule family time: leave work at work and home at home.
19. Touch ten people – prospects, customers, clients – every day in different ways.
20. Have fun all the time. Laugh, enjoy, grow.

Sales Coach International

Gerry Layo is the head sales coach/sales catalyst for Sales Coach International, where he wears two hats.

First, Gerry brings strong training to companies and associations throughout North America in the areas of sales and sales management. He does this through seminars, keynote addresses, and interactive workshops.

Second, Gerry heads up the coach programs for Sales Coach International, in which he, along with his exceptional group of coaches, works with many companies throughout North America on an ongoing basis as an outsourced sales manager and "coaches' couch". The companies involved in the SCI coach program have the benefit of not only working with Gerry and his coaches every month, but also of seeing dramatic improvements in their culture, systems, sales, and profits!

For the latest up-to-date information
and to receive continuous sales and sales
management tools and value, visit:
www.GerryLayo.com.